Copyright © 2020 Tekkan
Artwork Copyright © 2020

All rights reserved.
First Printing, 2020
ISBN 978-1-7343510-6-4

To contact Tekkan please email:
buddhaboy1289@gmail.com

This book is dedicated to my mother, Rema MacDonald, who is the source of the goodness I am capable of. — Tekkan

How to Read My Poems

I am an ordinary guy living a middle class life. I may imagine what it would be like to put on a wingsuit and jump off a mountain, but my stock-in-trade is the exploration of "everyday mind." I look for transcendent meaning in the ordinary happenings of daily life. I write in the morning everyday, and try to distill experience down to essentials. It is easy to overlook the instant-by-instant process of seeing, thinking, and responding to life — but in reality that is what life is.

The mind is self-interested and driven by powerful emotions. I look around and determine what to do. I judge what's worthy, and establish a list of priorities. My likes and dislikes become signposts, and if I am not careful I find myself repeating a pattern of behavior, and get stuck, narrowly seeing, feeling, experiencing — and then where is novelty?

Spring has sprung but today is chilly. I love watching the seasons change in a succession of little details, because the seasons are so much bigger than what's going on in my mind. There is always a lot going on in nature, and my practice is to open, so that more of reality may penetrate my consciousness.

I practice opening my awareness to the world inside and outside of me. Consciousness is a miracle — but I have to learn how to use the gift of Consciousness. This is what my poetry is about.

My daughter, Jocelyn MacDonald, is a wonderful artist. Her art work graces this book.

I am Barry MacDonald. I received the *dharma* name, *Tekkan*, which means, Iron Man, a settled practitioner of great determination.

— *Tekkan*

Everyday Mind VX

Puffs of dandelion seeds
little white spheres
scattered across the lawn
rising above the grass
are ready to go.

I got tired of watching the riders on
Fancy high-tech bicycles pass me by
So I purchased one with the stimulus
Money the government sent because of

The pandemic and on my first day I
Was going twice as fast only I have
To be careful in downtown Stillwater
Where people saunter around on foot and

Where I have to stop at the traffic lights
Because I'm using clip-on pedals and
Shoes that cost over a hundred dollars
And I am having fun zipping about but

Haven't got the hang of getting out of
The pedals so I brake and fall over.

Sitting at my desk
this morning I'm twisting
my ankle in pedal
disengagement mode
practicing.

For March April and May the barbershops
Have been closed because of the pandemic
Virus and they're opening on Monday
And thank God because the state of my hair

Is deplorable and I realize
On the scale of tragedy the weight of
Unappealing hair is wafer thin but
I want a return to normalcy and

And the persistent isolation of
Social distancing not allowing for
Conversation or for non-essential
Commerce is reaching the limit of its

Practicability and people are
Going to wig out if it doesn't end soon.

I've very tempted
to run the clipper
over my head but
I'm hesitant to
create divots.

In a chilly interlude within the
Warmer days of summer I noticed a
Blur in the air while mowing the grass that
With a more discerning attention turned

Out to be a dragonfly zigzagging
As only a dragonfly is able
With its four wings maneuvering forward
And backward and up and down and stopping

Suddenly and hovering in the air
Knowing as I do that a dragonfly has
Spherical eyes absorbing everything
About itself which makes me grateful that

I am not a fruit fly exposed to the
Predation of a true flying dragon.

Sunny summer brightness
goes very well with
the neon incandesce
of a dragonfly.

The onset of the pandemic virus
Three months ago forcing businesses to
Close and people to put their lives on hold
Was followed last week by the brutal and

Unjustified killing of a black man
By a white policeman prompting peaceful
Protests during the days and furious
Riots and lootings during the nights and

Americans are confused and angry
And divided with our major cities
Despoiled and burning with long simmering
Animosities igniting into

Warring factions with national guardsmen
Girding for a forceful intervention.

Society is revealed
as idealistic with
civilizing
institutions
sedately founded
upon latent volcanoes.

The video of a white policeman
Kneeling on the neck of a black man and
Killing him was a spark inflaming the
Outrage of Americans who believe

After all there is no racial justice
In America leading to a week
Of rioting and looting throughout the
Nation — and videos of black-garbed and

Masked thugs beating to unconsciousness the
Passersby or storeowners defending
Their property are broadcast once the sun
Goes down with darkness encouraging the

Violence of thugs that is always just
Around the corner and seeking an excuse.

Equality before the
law and justice are precious
American ideals
worthy of enforcing
in difficult times.

Early in the afternoon yesterday
A new humidity was in the air
With a haze obscuring a view of the
Distance southwards of the river valley

And the sun was beating on my arms as
I was clipped into the pedals pumping
My legs steadily pacing the incline
To the Crossing Bridge gripping the lower

Curls of the bicycle handles learning
To shift to the proper gear maintaining
My exertion at eighty percent of
Capacity aware of the dark clouds

Of an impending thunderstorm coming
With gusts from the northeast behind me.

This morning a
million drops of dew
are sparkling in the grass
with the rising sun.

The shards of conflicting opinions and
Passions have erupted into chaos
In cities with rioters destroying
Businesses and battling the police

And so many have a reason why the
Violence is necessary either
To address longstanding injustices
Or to defend lifetimes of effort while

Livelihoods and families are on the
Line as the opposing attitudes are
Hardening into concrete and voices
Of moderation are overwhelmed and

Will we find a resolution of our
Confusion or a just a simmering mess?

Certainly lies are
being told and politics
is a driving force but
who's to blame is
contestable.

It's not only the white peonies and
Dew drops on the grass that are worthy of
Celebrating this morning it's also
The sunlight that when I'm closing my eyes

And enjoying the quiet I'm noticing
The warmth of the sun inside my body
I'm seeing my eyelids are filtering
The light into the brightest shade of red

And I can pinpoint how high the sun is
As its rising by the intensity
Of it's heat giving me a sensation
To go with a perception of the peace

And I don't have to do anything or
To please anyone to earn the quiet.

Sensing the sun through my
closed eyelids enjoying
the heat radiating I
imagine myself a
tomato.

The splendor of our summer days presents
A face of reality I'd like to
Enjoy forever when the sun is a
Power browning my skin with its touch and

Warming the inside of my body and
When we can sleep with cool breezes with the
Windows open and on awakening
We can listen to the birds permeate

The air with song but soon mosquitoes will
Be biting and the humidity will
Be sweltering and the smallest tick is
Capable of imparting Lyme disease

And even as the roots of trees and grass
Are busy a barren season will come.

The face of reality
is like a weaving
of smoke
endlessly
fascinating.

As I'm sitting in the lotus posture
Quietly and with energy coursing
Through my body the assertion of a
Vigorous wind in the leaves becomes a

Dharma gate of curiosity as
I can hear the weight of injustice and
Cruelty in the mournful expression
Of the wind as if sorrowful questions

And grief are mixing in the blusters of
The leaves and the questions are unanswered
And I hear a lamentation in the
Wind rising upward to a crescendo

Of intensity and dissipating
Into surrendering despondency.

And yet there is also
consolation and
quiet within
the voices of the
wind in the leaves.

There is talk in our meetings about the
People in Wisconsin who aren't wearing
Masks and who are gathering in groups and
Are not keeping a safe distance between

Each other while we Minnesotans are
Seeing and hearing each other online
Within little boxes on screens with some
Of us scolding don't they know they can have

The virus without its symptoms spreading
It to vulnerable loved ones but I
Am enjoying the sun after such a
Chilly spring and I can close my eyes and

Know exactly where it is by its heat
Feeling a little dizzy and peaceful.

Pandemic virus
protests in cities
riots in cities with
most of us wearing
masks.

We got news from the United Nation's
World Health Organization that it is
Not likely that people with the virus
Without the symptomatic sneezing or

Coughing are in fact infecting other
People which undercuts the reasons why
Our leaders issued stay-at-home orders
And strangled our so-called nonessential

Businesses and shuttered the nation's schools
Which have never happened before and yet
Never mind it's only one opinion
Among many as no one knows for sure

And it's better safe than sorry except
For those whose livelihoods were destroyed.

Some of us can shrug
and laugh and others
can't while some are
getting sick and
dying.

The sky today is white like the pages
Of a book of poetry and in its
Whiteness is the essence of the oceans
And of waterfalls and springs in the way

Of metamorphoses and along the
Margins of the sky there are the millions
Of green leaves tossing in a wind with wind
And leaves cooperating and stirring

Crescendos of lyrical music that
Not everyone will notice but for those
Who listen the soundings are homilies
Consoling and soothing and there are no

Words embodied in the sky or in the
Meaning of the boisterous leafy wind.

The white pages of a
book of poetry are
full of words but the
words point beyond
the poetry.

I tap a finger on a key and a
Letter appears on the whiteness of the
Screen and the whiteness of the screen is like
The emptiness from which everything comes

And in the beginning there are spasms
Of thoughts that aren't cohering into a
Pattern worthy of expression as I
Put my chin on the heel of my hand while

Looking at the white of the screen waiting
For a direction that may bloom into
An inspiration that may form into
A poem that perhaps communicates

Something specific and meaningful to
Whomever may be reading it later.

But emptiness really
isn't white or black
and emptiness and
emanation come
together.

They have buckteeth that are propitious
For chewing wood and they like to climb and
Loiter in the trees making good use of
Their prehensile tails and if ever an

Animal could become a metaphor
For a period of history these
Are the creatures that serve the purpose as
When waddling along the ground they look

As inoffensive and vulnerable
As a squirrel or a rabbit but don't
Be so hasty as to venture a bite
Because they are extremely prickly

And you might find your snout impaled with
The needles and barbs of a porcupine.

Given the polarized
nature of America's
politics the porcupine
could serve as the nation's
emblem.

The days of life are like the layering
Of pages with the white of the paper
Being the light of possibility
And whoever notices the whiteness

And reliability of paper
Pages one following another as
Natural and as binding as the days
Of life as the substance of the paper

Was once the living trees absorbing the
Sunlight and drinking the water and the
Minerals of the soil as the whiteness
Of the paper is a reflection of

Sunlight and can you close your eyes over
The open pages and feel the sun's warmth?

There's a kinship between
the pages of my life
and the cottonwood
by my house flowing
in the wind.

In any room if one listens there is
A hum of electricity on the
Tipping point of consciousness as it takes
A ceasing of thoughts and a quietude

Of activity to hear the constant
Operation of machines channeling
Energy lighting our rooms cooling or
Heating space refrigerating our food

And in the distance there are power plants
Utilizing coal or natural gas
Or uranium marshaling a flow
Of electrical juice through a network

Of power lines crossing America
And into every solitary home.

We live like Kings
and yet through the
habit of comparison
we find reasons for
envy.

The elements of society are
Tensed and fractured into factions and the
News is a brew of shootings and riots
And accusatory narratives as

Ideals of justice and law enforcement
Are disintegrating as people are
Hating people who believe or who look
Different from them as the media

And politicos are spewing hateful
Words as they are whipping and driving the
Masses who they have hypnotized into
Fury surpassing moderation or

Introspection into a concoction
Of political opportunity.

One has to be wary
or belligerent to
express opinions
different from
the dominate narratives.

The riots and the pandemic are symptoms
Of human volatility and who
Could have predicted in December the
Cancellation of major league baseball

With owners and players disagreeing
On how to price a short season but I'm
Getting up early and applying the
Method of persistency crossing my

Legs and meditating in the midst of
Uncertainty and this morning I saw
Five almost identical crows cawing
And strutting together on my lawn and

When I stepped outside they scattered to the
Trees harshly complaining of my presence.

The blooms of pink roses
by my patio in the
morning light of June
are evidence of
continuity.

All the leaves have lost their springtime luster
The apple and lilac blossoms are gone
The resonance of the wind and the leaves
Is much less noticeable when it's hot

The heat is slowing the growth of the grass
And the afternoon sun is bearing down
Making the shade under the leaves welcome
And instead of the purple flowering

Of the Creeping Charlie the white blossoms
Of clover are predominant now and
The stems of little oval leaves and thorns
That are so easy to pass without thought

Are blooming within the humidity
In a collection of lovely roses.

Pink roses and
blooming clover
appear with the
summer heat
at my home.

An Ode to My Mentor — Cid Corman

By an old oak in Pioneer Park I
Discovered a stone on the ground that I
Absentmindedly picked up and handled
Turning it about until I noticed

A curve of it abutted my fleshy
Part below my thumb and another curve
Fit snugly within the cup of my hand
And it was small and round enough for my

Fingers to fold over the stone resting
My fingertips on the only flat part
Of the stone and there even happened to
Be a place for the tip of my pinky

Finger to rest — this random stone is a
Perfect match for the inside of my hand.

Holding the stone
warming the stone
imagining holding hands
I feel comprehended.

Kitcat lets me know when he's wanting the
Container of dry cat food that I keep
In the microwave by jumping onto
The microwave and pawing at a framed

Painting hanging above it and sometimes
He knocks the painting down so I'm compelled
To present the container to him in
The bathroom separate from Johnnie who

Isn't allowed the dry food and after
Kitcat is finished eating he pounds on
The door and yowls and I let him out
And then he rushes out — but as soon as

I put the container back inside the
Microwave he paws the painting again.

As Kitcat goes back
for a second helping
I suspect he's getting
a kick out of
bossing me around.

Summer Solstice

A cottonwood puff is rising in a breeze
And an eagle is skimming a crosswind
A lower cloud is moving northward while
The higher clouds are slowly going south

I heard numerous birds through the window
This morning in between my rising and
Dissipating thoughts and there was a dog
Barking in the distance and touching my

Ears but my mind kept returning to the
Accusatory currents of thoughts that
Are ricocheting across the Internet
Charging and countercharging racism

And I'm trying not to set what I think
Against what others believe I should think.

A poet said the great way
isn't difficult for
those who do not
pick and choose.

Sitting quietly without moving on
The grass he could be mistaken for a
Bumpy sort of rock but with a closer
View his squatting posture is apparent

And he looks like something that you wouldn't
Want to step on and mess your shoe with but
With a more careful look you can see his
Bulging eyes and his pudgy body and

He really is a funny-looking thing
Although his impassive face does bespeak
A degree of dignity and yet when
He flings himself forward with his springy

Rear legs he is so ridiculous
You wonder how this creature came to be.

I have outgrown
my childish urges
to grab and squish
a toad.

I do feel a little sorry for plants
Because they have so few choices to make
Passively accepting whatever comes
Sure they can extend their roots and flower

But they prosper or not depending on
Which side of the shady hill the seed falls
And on the consistency of the rain and
The sun and the minerals of the soil

And on the temperature — even so
There is a noble tenacity and
A splendid variety to behold
That with an intelligent pruning can

Produce an exquisite combination
Of thorns and irresistible beauty.

A red rose is as
iconic as the sun
and the moon.

Jason's Alternative View:

Plants create the hills the shade the living
Soil the carbon cycle the atmosphere
And the climate as they influence the
Starting and ending of the ice ages

Spreading their propagules throughout the earth
Choosing where and where not to germinate
In the conditions in which they can thrive
With orchid seeds and botrychium fern

Spores traveling in the jet stream to all
The corners of creation as the plants
Operate in a fundamentally
Different time frame than humans — which is

Their superpower their consciousness and
Their total planetary influence.

Plants use an abundance
of choice teaching us
to align ourselves with
the reality of our
cosmic incarnation.

(My friend Jason is an ecologist.)

Over fifteen years it has happened that
If I'm lying on my left side sleeping
I could wake any day with my left ear
Plugged with wax and because it happens so

Infrequently I muddle through pulling
On my earlobe extending my pinky
Fingertip down into my ear as far
As I can or tilting my head just so

In the shower to let the warm water
Stream directly into my ear canal
And it happens on the verge of panic
That the congealed wax will pop and my

Hearing is magically restored so
Then I can forget it ever happened.

But last night the wax
was determinedly
congealed and the
extension of panic
was lengthy.

A conflagration is spreading within
The big cities of America with
Mobs pulling down and dismembering the
Statues of statesmen as the mob isn't

Interested in the minutiae
Of history but they are inspired
With revolutionary fever to
Destroy American history and

Construct a radically different
Nation while the police are ordered to
Do nothing because the governors where
It's happening are accumulating

Political advantage from the mayhem
As a tacit way of attacking foes.

Using the leverage
of violent mobs is
as unpredictable
as lighting a grass fire
during a drought.

I don't want to argue with people who
Have different political views from
Me and yet because I cherish points of
View in opposition to others in

A time of conflagration I gather
The information to justify my
Reasoning being aware that I am
Cultivating passions and obsessing

Over the consequences of defeat
And victory immersing myself in
Battles without end and realizing
Humans have a way of painstakingly

Constructing a house of cards and in a
Pique of fury burning it to the ground.

In meditation I
pivot precariously
on the point of letting go
of thoughts and listening to
birds.

Now that the wax has been flushed from my ears
I can hear the sound of the rain within
My semi-consciousness and sleep and there
Is the kind of thunder that I haven't

Heard for years but a thunderous night is
An experience that one can never
Really forget and with every booming
Vibration there is an arching bolt of

Lightning illuminating a strange and
Ominous landscape full of tension and
Fear that I can only glimpse and every
Thundering impact is unique making

A dramatic but fleeting impression
In between the pattering of the rain.

The spattering of the
rain outlasts the
violence in the air
immersing anxiety
within a lullaby.

My clogs are much too big for my feet but
As long as I'm not walking in tall grass
And exposed to ticks and Lyme disease they are
The perfect form of summer shoe because

They have high heels and provide three inches
Of additional height and I don't have to
Bend over to tie a lace but just to
Slip into and out of them and on a whim

At my desk I can instantly achieve
Nakedness all the way up to my short
Pants while kneading the carpet with my toes
And yet when walking around town I am

Protected from bits of glass and gritty
Sand — striding about profoundly happy.

Only in summer
are my heels and ankles
and most of my feet
almost completely
liberated.

The roundness of a watermelon is
Challenging because it's slippery and
Hard to hold stationary with one hand
While cutting through the stubborn rind with the

Other but I'm clever so I put the
Watermelon inside the sink and use
The hole of the drain as a centering
Device that allows me to lustily

Saw into it with my watermelon
Knife that has very large and wicked teeth
And I don't have attend so much to
What my other hand is doing but I

Do find that the sides of the sink are an
Impediment to free-flowing motion.

Cutting off the tip of
my thumb I realize
I do have to attend
to what my other
hand is doing.

I have to overcome my resistance
To getting out of bed and wait until
The drowsiness of sleep dissipates but
Then I get to experience one of

The joys of living when my ideas
Start to pop like a bag of popcorn in
A microwave oven when I get to
Discover what was important about

What happened yesterday and how I feel
About a conversation and there are
Always words worth my pondering and then
I turn my attention to today and

Consider what I want to do and then
My energetic optimism comes.

I used to be so inside
of my thoughts that
I was blind to the
quality of my thoughts and
they ran away with me.

I am jubilant to see it on the
Way to Hudson as I'm driving over
The rise of a hill appearing with a
Cornfield and pasture next to a house a

Cattle barn and a corn silo and it
Doesn't look like it belongs there as its
Slender leaves are streaming in the wind as
It seems not only receptive but to be

The source of the wind and not merely to
Reflect but to emanate the sunlight
Standing out within its orderly and
Prosaic surroundings with its easy

Rippling and whispering in the wind as
A flaunting and flourishing touch of grace.

I forget all about it
until I crest the hill and
am captured again
in quiet celebration
of the willow tree.

I remembered the story of the Zen
Master who asked the monk — what is it that
Comes to talk to me — and the monk paused and
Then he turned and walked away because he

Could not answer the riddling question
And he knew that the master would ask
Until he had a satisfactory
Reply and I remembered the master's

Question as I was walking away from
My friends after our conversation as
They were continuing to listen and
To speak and I asked myself what is it

That comes and goes and listens and speaks and
Wherever it goes the world is changing?

And there is always
more going on
in every direction
than can possibly be
comprehended.

In every day at any time of the
Day and it's especially true when the
Summer heat is lingering through the night
And into the morning and sapping my

Energy that there does happen to be
A little listlessness to be managed
And if not managed could well become a
Pool of apathy to wallow within

But I can close my eyes when facing the
Sun and see my eyelids turn red with the
Sunlight and I can linger within the
Heat of the sunlight and listen to the

Hum of electricity in the room
And then there is only me and the sun.

Dazzling energy
penetrates my red eyelids
apart from notions
of urgency making me
just a little dizzy.

I saw a busy little bumblebee
Bobbing about the clover of my grass
Within a carefree summer afternoon
And it really wasn't entirely

Without care as I had to mow the grass
And whack the grass around the rock gardens
And pick up the twigs my cottonwood drops
And spray some herbicide on pesky weeds

But once I begin bumbling about
Doing one thing after another does
Become a moving and a merging of
Mindless activity and so I feel

That the bee and me are simpatico
Following a simple program of chores.

I wonder what the bee
is thinking as my
thoughts are busy with
trivialities.

The prank of slathering words on a screen
And finagling each word to cohere
Into a packet of clarity that
May survive to decorate the pages

Of a book doesn't come as simply as
It appears as the perpetual state
Of my mind resembles a Mexican
Jumping Bean of chaotic random thoughts

And it's propitious to pause enough
To permit the right word to penetrate
And settle in a proper arrangement
Somewhat like old-fashioned photography

As the camera needs a long exposure
To propound a poetic palaver.

A calico cat
leaped onto my lap
in the middle of
this poem.

It is a presidential election
Year and I have only to turn on the
Radio while driving for five minutes
To hear excited voices disputing

A current controversy to be caught
Again in the furious world of us
Versus them — whereas I had come from a
Moment in the park where I saw a bird

Flitting and coasting through the air and I
Also heard it cheeping as it flew and
The sky was as clear and blue as could be
With only a crescent moon to be seen

As the leaves were lit by the rising sun
And bird song punctuated the breezes.

I have perfect freedom
to navigate between
the stridency of
humanity or
evanescence.

I don't agree with the snobs who think that
The plastic flamingos that people in
Minnesota sprinkle their yards with are
Crass or gaudy because the color pink

Is incandescent and goes very well
With a summer afternoon when the blue
Of the sky and the white of the clouds and
The green of the grass are all shining with

The nourishing sun and it's true that the
Form of a synthetic flamingo or
A flock of plastic flamingos aren't on
A par with Michelangelo's David

But the audacity and flamboyance
Of hosting pink flamingos is worthy.

The flamingos are
a tonic to the eyes
and a taste of the
exotic.

Do you feel the momentum in the air
In the month of July when the sun is
Burning the air with its touch and all the
Leaves are receptive and drinking in the

Radiance as if the trees were sailing
Ships with every sail aloft and full of
The force of the wind and the fire of the
Orb is penetrating stimulating

And scorching the skin and the blue of the
Sky is overwhelmed with the pulsation
Of descending heat and every kind of
Flower is in kaleidoscopic bloom

And the shade under the trees is welcome
As an oasis from the blazing sun?

A white t-shirt
becomes a blazing
emblem of
summer frolic
and liberation.

Some of us stubbornly believe somewhere
Out in the woods there is the disheveled
Giant that we dub with the sobriquet
Big Foot and he is a shy and slippery

Fellow almost always evading our
Scientific verification and
He surely possesses a prodigious
Intellect otherwise how could he have

Eluded an eager hunter's bullet
For all these years and I have considered
Having seen the one grainy snippet of
A video of him striding away

Swinging his arms that he could do with a
Vigorous combing out of ticks and fleas.

I've been told that
we don't find any
Big Foot residue
because porcupines
eat his bones.

Once the gyms were closed in the spring because
Of the pandemic I had to find a
Different way of exercising and
The simplest method is to lift the

Weight of my body as if I were a
Dumbbell so I started doing sit-ups
And push-ups hundreds of times and it is
Frustrating because my mind wanders and

I lose count of the repetitions so
How many I do are probably more
Or less than I think I've done and in the
Process it's amazing where my mind will

Wander as I am becoming obsessed
With the supreme importance of my toes.

Did you know
when doing push-ups
the tiny tips of big toes
become essential
balancing points?

My laser printer needs an adjustment
As every now and then it will run through
Two sheets of paper instead of one and
I regret the waste of paper but not

Enough to hire someone to fix it and
So I use the curved sheets that cannot be
Processed through the printer again without
Jamming as notepaper for writing down

The spelling of names or for the exact
Wording of phrases or to record an
Instant inspiration for a poem
And I am writing many notes on each

Single sheet of paper and the pile of
Paper is slowly accumulating.

I look at the pile of
clean and exactly cut
sheets of paper ready for
use as the epitome
of civilization.

I haven't run out of surprising things
To see this summer as everywhere I'm
Driving wildflowers and hydrangeas are
Catching my eye as luscious accent points

In my day and I can't calculate how
Many years I've wasted attending to
A crazy monologue in my head and
Sometimes there are two of me debating

Fractious controversies devolving to
Indecision and all the while beyond
My thinking there is a festival to
Be experienced bearing down on me

From every direction meeting me more
Than halfway and ready to transform me.

I live in a cosmos
of supernovas
of black holes
of wildflowers
of hydrangeas.

The leaves are not themselves complete without
The sunlight radiating upon them
And the blue of the atmosphere is not
An item existing by itself but

The atmosphere is a co-creator
With the earth and the sun and the oceans
And I don't believe the boundary of
My skin separates me from the swirl of

Life as every breath is an exchange of
Essence and I popped into consciousness
Not making any distinctions about
Distances and I could very well have

Reached my hands upward to possess the moon
To become mystified by its presence.

I didn't invent these words
but I am playing with them
and am playing at
understanding.

It was a surprising observation
Once the car was going on the highway
To see a tree frog plastered onto the
Windshield resisting the force of the wind

With its toes splayed on the glass and body
A study of stoic resolution
For what was it to do otherwise than
To hold on for dear life and so the frog

Became an emblem of anyone who
Is caught without warning in perilous
Circumstances impelled forward to an
Unknown destination leaving behind

Comfortable familiarity
And straining every fiber to stay put.

It's astounding
such a puny
squishy creature
with bug eyes
has so much pluck.

What does a cornfield extending into
The distance with an empty sky on
The horizon mean to you if you stop
To question it — and there is often a

Line of coniferous trees sheltering
A homestead from the wind in the country —
However far one looks there is always
A boundary of the sky and the earth —

On occasion a wisp of cloud becomes
Visible — do you take the time to watch
It blow and change its shape — you may see the
Pace of metamorphosis if you do —

Even the emptiness of the sky is
Tricky as it's really filled with sunlight.

No eyes / no sun
no ears / no rain
no skin / no coolness
no nose / no roses
no tongue / no watermelon
no mind / then what?

To be and to spread its leaves every year
Sedately growing on a limestone bluff
Overlooking downtown Stillwater and
Set high above the wide flowing river

The oak is reaching upwards to the sun
Growing acorns and spreading its branches
Expanding its girth in every season
Its roots drinking minerals and water

It was growing when the American
Frontier passed by and a lumber baron
Built a mansion next to it but now the
Building is gone while it is flourishing

There used to be steamboats on the river
And lumberjacks came into town for fun.

The oak adds a touch of
majesty to its home
in Pioneer Park on
the northwards bluff of
Stillwater Minnesota.

Memory is weighty before the dawn
When I'm weary and reluctant to move
When my mind is busy remembering
My marriage and my rambunctious children

When there was so much living yet to do
With so many things to look forward to
And with decades of possibility
But now I have my cats for company

As my kids are pursuing their own dreams
And I would rather let the memories
Go but it's apparent that how I am
Remembering is beyond my control

In the early hours of the morning
When I feel the weight of what has happened.

I enjoy energy
listening to birds
through the window
while meditating
in the morning.

Before I bought a racing bicycle
I was riding a clunker and had to
Watch in frustration as other riders
With better bikes would pass me by but now

When a rider is bold enough to pass
Then he becomes a rabbit whom I chase
And I don't want to catch him because then
I would become the rabbit but what I

Want is to prove to myself that I can
Follow the best of them up the steepest
Hill or along a rising gradient
Against the wind and I've been successful

With the guys with fancy jerseys and bikes
Until I encountered Doug from the gym.

Doug is a
knowledgeable
modest friendly
smiling fellow who
left me far behind.

Yes we're in the latter half of July
And even though the light is sparkling in
The cottonwood leaves well into evening
I'm beginning to notice a mellow

Golden touch about the sunlight and I
Also saw while driving around town my
First sightings of the paling of the green
Leaves into shadings of red and yellow

And maybe I'm falling into a mood
And looking for reasons to be gloomy
As year after year I've trained myself to
Specify the descent into winter

While I could enjoy the open windows
And cool mornings and the hot afternoons.

There is always a tinge
of February in
Minnesota — light in
July but harsh in
March April and May.

I enjoy an hour of sanctuary
At my desk for playing with words apart
From the madness of current events as
Vitriol and accusation is out

Of control with riots continuing
For two months in Portland while dozens of
People are being shot every weekend
In Chicago as children are being

Killed in homes and cars by the stray bullets
Involved in gang warfare and parental
Heartbreak is useful for fabricating
Political narratives but the threads

Of societal disease are tangled
Almost beyond honest comprehension.

It's much easier
to specify an enemy
to foment a rage
to seek advantage
than to comprehend.

I was walking on a cool afternoon
And entered the grounds of a neighborhood
Temple in Kyoto when no one else was
About and I came upon the bell and

I held the beam hanging on a chain and
I swung the beam backward and forward and
Struck the bell and the sound resonated
In the air slowly and deeply and I

Felt the vibration pulsating within
My ears and the reverberation was
Continuous in somber crests and troughs
And I've never heard anything like it

And I don't completely understand it
But it sounded both solemn and joyful.

I might say the
temple bell continues
to reverberate as a
summons on a
threshold.

I would rather not be an amateur
Psychologist especially when it
Comes to deciphering the behavior
Of my cat but I can't tolerate the

Odor of cat urine when entering
My home and I've met him more than halfway
Provided him with another litter
Box taking me twice the time for cleaning

Yet he seems to delight in peeing not
Inside but all around the litter box
And things can't continue as they are as
I'd be ashamed to bring home visitors

Yet moral exhortation wouldn't work
When Kitcat is incapable of shame.

I admit a little
observation goes
a long way as the
litter box is too little
and Kitcat is too big.

I scatter poems about me printing
Copies and forgetting where I leave them
And my Mom came upon the previous
Poem and in alarm she provided

Me with cleaning canisters and strongly
Discouraged the publication of the
Poem and I accepted the supplies
And thanked her but she doesn't know that I've

Already read the poem to several
Friends and have given and received just what
I wanted — a laugh — and this morning I
Received the continuing expression

Of my mother's concern and affection
And that's an inspiration for today.

Kitty residue
is manageable
but a mother's love
is indestructible.

My Mom has always been good at growing
Plants inside the house taking care to find
A fitting placement with a sufficient
Amount of sunshine for each of them and

Outside she exercises a distaste
For dandelions by patrolling the
Lawn with a bucket and picker even
Though she is over eighty years old and

The home and property where my siblings
And I were raised and where our children and
Even their children are visiting will
Be remembered as a sanctuary

Of love in the form of geraniums
Of pansies marigolds and yellow bells.

Santa Barbara
Bemidji Galveston
Oxford and Kyoto
were my temporary
domiciles but not
home.

Each of my poems is following a
Formula by launching a miniature
Narrative and I am intending to
Intrigue and ensnare my readers with my

Initial words compelling them to press
Forward and it's a game to engender
Expectations using ordinary
Words and everyday experience in

Unusual ways and it's a riot
In the middle to change directions as
If the reader suddenly comes upon
A turning without a clue about what's

Around the corner and then I have a
Big laugh by delivering a punch line.

The truth is I often start
writing with vague ideas
not knowing where
I'm going or how
to get there.

I keep the rock that fits perfectly in
My hand upon my desk and hold it in
My palm and appreciate its weight and
Solid substance and with my fingertips

I evaluate its roundness and smooth
Texture and I raise it to my nostrils
With both of my hands and inhale to smell
Just the slightest scent of what may be

The essence of the stone or of perhaps
The lingering scent of the soil and I
Press it against my cheek as another
Way of touching it and realize that

The stone and I are fellow travelers
Coincidentally brought together.

Both of us will return
To soil but the rock will
More stubbornly preserve
its form.

Is there a word or a phrase that captures
The background of things that includes yet goes
Beyond the shade of a maple tree and
The interweaving of its branches and

Leaves that I mean resembles the sunlight
The atmosphere and even the cosmos
But is bigger than that because it does
Encompass the process of becoming

On the scale of geologic time or
The momentary transformation of
A cloud and in which every perception
And emotion I might have within a

Conversation plays its part — is there a
Word or a phrase that contains everything?

In all directions
everything is
transforming
and it's happening
now.

By practicing a steady cadence on
My bicycle without straining I can
Overcome a headwind and I enjoy
The swallows flitting from the overpass

Beyond the bridge and the killdeer startled
By my passage at the top of the hill
While further on by fields of soybeans and
Corn I notice monarch butterflies and

Grasshoppers and yellow moths and when I
Turn about for home I can rely on
A swelling slope of purple thistles to
Cheer me on and then I take a purely

Superfluous loop around a parking
Lot to listen to the chirping insects.

Sun-drenched
afternoons and
simple carefree
sweaty exertion
is glorious.

It's a relief not to be arguing
Anymore and bearing the burden that
Comes with a marriage that wasn't working
For decades and I am adapting to

The solitude of living by myself
Not having to inhibit or adjust
My behavior for another person's
Presence while I am communicating

With my cats more frequently than not with
Nonverbal exclamations that they seem
To understand yet I'm discovering
The importance of conversation with

My friends providing the give and take of
Perspectives — keeping my spirit supple.

Kitcat and I took naps
Saturday afternoon
on our backs
with our limbs
stretched carelessly.

Scientists are learning more about the
Dynamics of the event horizons
Of black holes but I don't suppose they are
Concerned about the moment happening

Now and its connection with what is called
Consciousness that can be separated
Into bits for analysis such as
Sensation and association and

Memory and volition but for me
Happiness depends upon my poise in
The moment enabling me to see
Without distraction the motion within

Oak leaves caused by excitable squirrels
While clouds are quickly moving to the south.

Is
consciousness
inside
the
moment
or
is
the
moment
inside
consciousness?

My Apple mouse stopped working because its
Cord got frayed so I traipsed to Office Max
For a replacement and discovered a
Cordless version providing untethered

Freedom of movement to go along with
The instant spell check that I'm used to and
There's a roller on top of the mouse that
Enables me to raise and lower the

Essays I'm reading online and I'm pleased
Beyond my expectations of the things
I can do with my fingertips and yet
Wherever I go and whatever I

Do on the Internet I'm still engaged
With the same old squabbling humanity.

Twenty years from now
the pile of words composed
above will become
gibberish except for
the bit about people.

I have upon my desk a replica
Version of "Sting" the small sword that Frodo
Carried into Mordor and I have the
Curved blade that Aragon was given in

Lothlorien by the queen of the elves
Galadriel and I know from reading
Tolkien that both of these weapons were forged
In the hidden kingdom of Gondolin

In the First Age of Middle Earth before
It was betrayed and destroyed by dragons
And demons and yet the blades survived to
Carry on into the War of the Rings

In the Third Age of Men when Frodo threw
The One Ring into the fire of Mount Doom.

Blades are passé
compared with
stealth airplanes
intercontinental
missiles and
battlefield lasers.

Dear Reader I'm sorry I played a trick
On you in the previous pages by
Implying that words are capable of
Containing anything other than mere

Ideas because the best that I can
Do is to point a shaky finger in
The correct general direction of
Something tangible in the real world but

You by yourself are responsible for
Making the leap of realization
Based on your own experience bearing
Upon your sincerity of purpose

Depending on your curiosity
Believing there is something to be known.

And yet straining and
staring to discover
something that's just
beyond grasping is
self-defeating.

I asked whether consciousness is inside
The moment or whether the moment is
Inside consciousness but perhaps those are not
Propitious questions as there may not

Be an inside or outside quality
Appropriate to the questions and it's
Better to believe that consciousness and
The moment arise together and then

Dissolve without each other and perhaps
They aren't separate things at all but are
One phenomenon which to me becomes
An optimistic point of view because

The implication is that consciousness
Continues beyond personality.

Is it possible
to imagine
the absence of
the moment
and consciousness?

My consciousness was occupied with an
Unpleasant dilemma last night on the
Verge of falling asleep as I became
Aware of a mosquito whining near

And far from my ear as I attempted to
Swat it but only hit my ear and I
Turned on the light but couldn't see it and
I remembered Jason's advice after

A similar incident to let it
Bite and I attempted to do so but
The resulting tension kept me from sleep
Waiting for a sting that didn't come as

I would rather have been thinking about
Anything else but I couldn't escape.

My consciousness
and the mosquito's
consciousness
were at
cross-purposes.

I gave an outside thermometer to
My father twenty years ago as a
Christmas gift with the image of the King
Of Rock n' Roll the crooner with the leer

The tousled hair and the gyrating hips
And Elvis was slouching in a golden
Suit and shirt and tie and he was even
Wearing golden shoes as a deserving

Celebration of his one hundred ten
Gold Records appearing as I supposed
The symbol of the initiation
Of the destruction of American

Culture and ever since the days of the
King the whole damn country has gone to Hell.

I suppose I'll take
the thermometer
out of its cardboard and
plastic wrappings and
use it myself.

I'm wearing a wide-brim straw hat as a
Shield from the sun and the weave of it is
Porous allowing many specks of light
To pass when the sun emerges from the

Clouds and the sky is a panoply of
Airy visions this morning as a bank
Of clouds high in the distance is fringed with
Sun looking like a heavenly mountain

But with a glance away and back again
I see predominantly gray clouds with
Feathery white edges and with rays of
The light visible and seeing the sweep

Of the sky I think the clouds are moving
Eastward but later I'm supposing north.

An occasional
clearing of the clouds
lights the brim of my hat
with brilliance.

The danger in playing with words is that
One could easily become serious
About it when going to poetry
Workshops and subjecting one's prize object

Of creativity to scrutiny
When everyone in turn can have a say
About whether an image works or a
Phrase could have been stronger or perhaps the

Use of enjambment is discordant but
I participate because I want to
Know whether my listeners or readers
Are actually understanding me

Because like trapeze artists we poets
Like to take leaps and hope that we are caught.

A bruised ego
along with a
playful attitude
is fertile ground.

There is such a big difference between
Reading the poem silently on a
Page to oneself and hearing the poem
Read by the poet and having only

Vibrations of sound to go by as the
Eye will be measuring the poem in
The form of words and lines and taking the
Luxury to linger and look deeper

While when listening to a poem the
Significance of the breaking and turning
Of the lines disappears and the rhythm
And the meaning become paramount and

The effect is instantaneous and
All that matters is the poem's impact.

The ear measures a poem
in the easy flow of words
within a series of
breaths.

When I hold a glass of water I can
See the absence of color and when I
Drink the water I can taste its tasteless
Quality and yet it is nourishing

Morning clarity has the same sort of
Character for me once the drowsiness
Of sleep is over as I can enjoy the
Lack of anxiety and weariness

I can see and hear the activity
Of the birds and when the cars drive by they
Reverberate and when the wind is up
The leaves are sighing and my mind isn't

Caught in resentments or worried about
The details I have no way to influence.

It's taken many decades
to appreciate the
absence of
anxiety and
agitation.

A conclusion is hanging in the air
As the apples are falling from my tree
As the sun is not as fierce as it was
And the days begin with mellow coolness

And I have lost track but it seems lately
We have so frequently begun our days
With cloudless glorious skies and mild suns
Only to be overcome by rainy

Afternoons and I must admit to an
Element of weariness about the
Endless repetitions of the seasons
As I know the days will never be more

Temperate and beautiful than now and
I really do love these quiet mornings.

Hearing crows
through my open window
punctuates
enveloping
quiet.

It's better to have a nerdy flair for
The boring details of policy to
Appreciate the glorious show of
Politics but what's absolutely key

To be a powerful politico
Is a passion for gossip and high school
Drama with a zest for secrecy and
A genius for twisting data into

Useful fables while smiling sincerely
As the creation of a comforting
Trustworthy and attractive persona
With a hint of savvy rascality

Will sway the masses of the ignorant
And capture the hearts of the gullible.

The henchmen
of democracy
are nasty but
they don't rise
to the top.

I've acquired a taste for the game of
Politics savoring verbosity
And pageantry appreciating how
Elections become the central drama

Of our culture anticipating the
Precarious balancing of power
Witnessing a truth of human nature
That audacity seizes victory

But it's also true that deception and
Power are inextricable and most
Of our politicos are selfishly
Motivated and that they are content

To exchange one pernicious policy
For an equally lousy solution.

It becomes more
difficult over the years
to tolerate the many
commonplace
lies.

I am a clever writer conniving
With co-conspirators propagating
A political agenda at odds
With the dominant ideology

Publishing a journal of opinion
With writers throughout America with
The goal of preserving liberty
Against totalitarianism

But ours is a big country with many
Divisions working at cross-purposes
And it's easier to assassinate
An opponent's character in the press

Than to explain the complexity of
Issues so we have to be circumspect.

I have the liberty
not to talk or
argue about
politics with my
family and friends.

I wheeled my container of garbage to
The curb to be picked up the next morning
And the sky was navy blue before the
Dawn and I saw a crescent moon and the

Stars glittering in luminosity
And I thought of the Chinese river and
Mountain poets alone within the wild
Country preferring isolation to

The stridency of civilization
And I wondered whether it was worth the
Loneliness to dedicate their lives to
Unhindered unfiltered experience

Listening to resonant waterfalls
Gazing at the luminous crescent moon?

The August sun
going down is a
mellow orange
and the light
on the leaves
is golden.

Last year I raked together the fallen
Apples and stooped over picking them up
And dropping the apples into lawn bags
For Waste Management to dispose of — which

Is tedious and laborious and
Lacking in dignity which prompted me
To question — why am I doing this — with
The answer being because otherwise

The neighbors will think that I'm untidy
And I realized maybe they think so
And maybe not but why should I care so
This year the apples are fermenting in

The grass providing a feast for rabbits
And squirrels and a festival of bugs.

There are only so many
apples I can eat before
they rot and apples in
lawn bags are surprisingly
heavy.

Yesterday was tainted by the threat of
An early evening storm and the vigor
Of the wind in the early afternoon
Was harsh diminishing my frolic on

My bicycle so I came home early
Anticipating intensifying
Blusters and the onset in twilight was
Overwhelming with the rain and the wind

Roaring in my cottonwood with all of
The branches flailing about as I rushed
To close my west windows while I relished
The calamitous clapping of thunder

But within five minutes it was over
And I was disappointed wanting more.

Some of the strewn cottonwood
branches on my lawn
will need to be sawed
and they won't ferment so
I need to bag them.

I share my house with Johnnie
Who is a rapacious beast
He yowls for his food
Three times in a day
Demanding another feast.

I also live with Kitcat
Who is reliably nuts
Learning from Johnnie
He yowls for his food
But then he refuses to eat.

A fly is only a fly and not worth
My noticing but Kitcat is thinking
Otherwise as he's encompassed within a
Little house and is able to see through

The windows rabbits munching grass and birds
Darting in the air but he can only
Express his energy by scrambling through
The rooms leaping into the air onto

Furniture with acrobatic aplomb
And today he was doing a dance by
Standing up on his haunches balancing
With his tail and swatting with his front paws

As an enticing and elusive object
Of joy provided meaning to his life.

I'm sure by now
he's familiar with
the taste of
flies.

I notice the way we poets employ
A straight left margin and I emphasize
Its rigidness with capital letters
And I also adhere to a form by

Utilizing ten syllables a line
And for me these devices are symbols
For the way we humans organize our
Lives separating our experience

Into minutes hours days weeks and months
And how could we do otherwise because
Segmentation is inherent in us
But I don't give a damn whether my lines

End with insignificant words because
That allows for flowing exploration.

I enjoy the tension
generated between
discipline and
spontaneity.

It's better to be grateful even in
February in Minnesota than
To be glum when the icy snow arrives
Because the sun is a welcome blessing

Throughout the year with a rainbow spectrum
Of appearances and even on a
Cloudy day in winter the sun lights the
Earth while we could be set within the blaze

Of the perpetually drifting sands
Of the Sahara without rivers and
Trees where the sun is a menace rising
Over the horizon broiling every

Grain of sand compelling every thought to
Endurance — baking every molecule.

The sun in Minnesota
is mild enough
to raise a garden
paradise.

Driving around town amidst the golden
Light of August I am seeing many
Kinds of riding lawnmowers of a sort
That specializes in taking care of

Swaths of grass between offices or on
A golf course and if I were so employed
I'd prefer the type in which the rider
Is standing rather than sitting because

Over every rise and hollow would be
The sensation of riding the swells and
Troughs of the fluctuating ocean and
I'd like to be rising and falling and

Flexing my knees pirouetting around
Trees and manhandling those swirling blades.

I wouldn't have to
think about anything
other than delusions
of grandeur.

I have a comforting memory of
Camping with my family when I was
A child of watching the wind making the
Leaves of a single slender poplar tree

Sigh as I was impacted by the grace
Of the turning leaves and of the swaying
Of the tree as something inside of me
Responded saying here is peace and this

Is beautiful and there really is no
Reason to be afraid or upset with
The chaotic appearances of things
Because underneath it all there is a

Gentleness and a harmony that the
Mind of a quiet child can recognize.

Now and then
without conscious effort
the image of the poplar
in the wind
reemerges.

I know Doug from the gym and he urged me
To ditch the stationary bike and spend
My saved-up money on a genuine
Road bicycle and so this summer I

Did and we aren't conniving to meet but
It's happening that on the trails we are
Coming across each other and he's the
Veteran and there was a day he left

Me behind but I'm stubborn and I use
The method of persistency and we've
Taken to racing up the hill into
Houlton rising off our seats to sprint to

The top and he usually wins but
Yesterday I managed to edge him out.

We are a couple
of roving sports
bypassing
dilettantes and
sluggards.

I saw a slender tree in the wind with
Its leaves turning and sighing with the breeze
When I was young enough not to have a
Developed vocabulary so I

Didn't know it was a poplar tree and
Couldn't have said why it was peaceful and
Beautiful but that momentary sight
Of a single tree swaying in a breeze

Has grown deep roots within me as the tree
Was there that day to give me and only
Me a vision embedding hints inside
Of me that even though there is such

Awful striving in life I can find a
Way to drop the stress and be full of peace.

To a child's eyes
visions come
unfiltered by
experience.

Yesterday was a good day to be shown
That no matter how good I think I am
Another cyclist will probably come
From behind and pass me by as happened

On the arduous hill to Houlton but
Smelling the cow manure at the top
Flying downward over the Crossing Bridge
To the long decline into Stillwater

Savoring the liberation of speed
Seeing the sunflowers and wildflowers
Hearing the crickets from within the grass
Watching afternoon shadows lengthen was

Worth my pedaling the circuit over
And over again until my crotch hurt.

The pinnacle
of summer
is worthy of
exhaustion
mixed with
satisfaction.

I bicycle over two bridges and
Around a river valley while at the
Same time the earth is rotating on its
Axis and orbiting the sun of our

Solar system and our solar system
Is not idle but is orbiting a
Spiraling galaxy that we call the
Milky Way and the Milky Way isn't

Idle either as it's moving away
From whatever happened that we call the
Big Bang however long ago that was
And where the Milky Way is going is

Hard to say except that it's expanding
Amidst trillions of other galaxies.

So I'm a speck
on a bicycle
cycling within cycles
pedaling who knows
where?

During the t-shirt and short pants days of
Summer it's difficult to imagine
The absence of the leaves even though I've
Seen the bare branches of winter for year

After year and I've heard the lamenting
Wind in the naked trees — and even on
The coldest overcast February
Morning it's tricky to imagine the

Absence of the sun because then the day
Would be in total darkness and the cold
Would be even colder — and it's even
Trickier to imagine the absence

Of the earth because there would be nowhere
To stand without the slightest gust of wind.

Perhaps it's impossible
but try to imagine
the absence of everything
which is the emptiness
from which we come.

There's a corner of the windowsill where
I can see the gossamer threads of a
Spider's web but I am usually
Cogitating about writing something

And seeing clouds and leaves is expansive
But gazing at the corner is boring
And it takes effort to rise from my chair
To get a paper towel and clean it up

But the other day I actually
Saw a delicate and spindly spider
Spinning another thread and I thought how
Diligent and admirable and how

Worthy of my attention and I can
See him now hanging quite motionless.

Later I will curl
fifty-pound dumbbells
twenty-five times in a row
but I'll probably leave
the spider alone.

It would be tricky to see because it
Moves about at night and it resembles
An oversized rat with an extremely
Elongated nose culminating with

What looks like a pig's snout that really is
An excellent sniffer and maybe its
Most salient attribute is its most
Adroit and lengthy tongue capable of

Catching its skittering prey and I do
Puzzle over how a creature with such
Equipment could manage to swallow but
Somehow it does and it trots around on

Four powerful legs with sharp claws that are
Superb for defense and for burrowing.

Besides being one of the
first words appearing in the
dictionary it's odd
because who could invent
the name — aardvark?

Why anyone would want to do such a
Thing that goes against every instinct is
Truly beyond me as I discovered
Last year that such mild activity as

Swinging my partner in a line dance would
Make me dizzy surpassing the point of
Nausea but to tether one's foot to
A cord and jump from the safety of a

Bridge and plunge headlong through a depth only
To be stopped and jerked upward again by
A bungee cord as the jumper must be
An adrenaline junkie addled with

Insanity without a sense of grace
Willing to impersonate a yo-yo.

To be bag of bones
and innards depending
on the elasticity of
any random cord
is bonkers.

Summer is the season for the city
To excavate the streets upgrading the
Concrete drainage system and they are not
Replacing the entire street but they

Are doing patch work and complicating
An already hodgepodge surface that makes
Me maneuver down a side street a block
Beside my usual route exploring

Houses and yards I've never seen after
Living in Stillwater for decades and
I could be driving about in any
Town USA and it's remarkable

To recognize how much like a mouse in
A comfortable maze that I've become.

The city has an army
of trucks and treaded
vehicles with different
kinds of steel shovels
and pulverizing tools.

The city snowplow has its opposite
Once the weather starts to rain again and
The street sweeper is the oddest-looking
Vehicle being boxy in the front

And tapering to a point with only
One double wheel behind and the purpose
Of the contraption is to clear the street
Of the accumulated grit and bits

Of glass and of the twigs and leaves that are
Constantly present because nobody
Else but the city is assuming the
Responsibility and without the

Periodic operation of the
Sweeper we'd all be living in a dump.

Angled disks on both sides
of the city sweeper
swirl bristles around
and around making
life tolerable.

At the garden section of Home Depot
Twenty years ago I bought two apple
Trees without any knowledge about the
Variety of types and presently

My choices are bearing fruit as one of
Them is generating yellow and soft
Apples at the end of July but the
Other is providing crisper red and

Yellow apples ripening finally
In September and I'm happy with the
Yellow apples because they are tasty
But the later red and yellow ones are

Bitter and hard and maybe the rabbits
And squirrels can digest them but not me.

Like politicians
the nature of the
apple tree is
revealed
eventually.

The bitter and hard apples
take longer to become
mush and dissolve into
the earth but it does
happen.

— Tekkan

www.ingramcontent.com/pod-product-compliance
Lightning Source LLC
Chambersburg PA
CBHW042118100526
44587CB00025B/4104